✳ ✳ ✳ ✳ ✳ ✳ ✳ ✳ ✳ ✳ ✳ ✳ ✳ ✳ ✳ ✳ ✳ ✳ ✳

*"Many women do noble things,
but you surpass them all."*

For you, Grandma

_____

with love,

_____

date

_____

✳ ✳ ✳ ✳ ✳ ✳ ✳ ✳ ✳ ✳ ✳ ✳ ✳ ✳ ✳ ✳ ✳ ✳ ✳

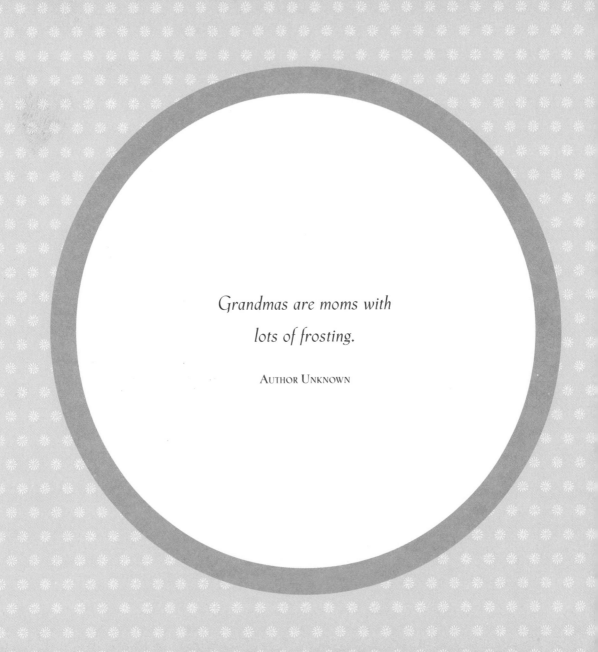

Grandmas are moms with

lots of frosting.

AUTHOR UNKNOWN

The
BEST
GRANDMA
in the **WORLD**

HOWARD BOOKS
A DIVISION OF SIMON & SCHUSTER
New York   London   Toronto   Sydney

Our purpose at Howard Books is to:

- *Increase faith* in the hearts of growing Christians
- *Inspire holiness* in the lives of believers
- *Instill hope* in the hearts of struggling people everywhere

Because He's coming again!

Published by Howard Books, a division of Simon & Schuster, Inc.
1230 Avenue of the Americas, New York, NY 10020
www.howardpublishing.com

The Best Grandma in the World © 2007 by Dave Bordon & Associates, LLC

Library of Congress Cataloging-in-Publication Data

The best grandma in the world / [edited by Chrys Howard].
   p. cm.
 Includes bibliographical references.
 ISBN-13: 978-1-4165-4174-5
 ISBN-10: 1-4165-4174-8
 ISBN-13: 978-1-58229-694-4 (gift ed.)
 ISBN-10: 1-58229-694-4 (gift ed.)
 1. Family—Religious aspects—Christianity. 2. Grandmothers—Family relationships. 3. Grandmothers—Religious life. I. Howard, Chrys, 1953–
 BT707.7.B47 2007
 242'.6431—dc22
               2007015583
10 9 8 7 6 5 4 3 2 1

Manufactured in the United States of America

For information regarding special discounts for bulk purchases, please contact: Simon & Schuster Special Sales at 1-800-456-6798 or business@simonandschuster.com.

Project developed by Bordon Books, Tulsa, Oklahoma
Project writing and compilation by Shawna McMurry and Christy Phillippe in association with Bordon Books
Edited by Chrys Howard
Cover design by Lori Jackson, LJ Design

CONTENTS

WHAT ARE GRANDMAS FOR?

Grandmas are for stories
   about things of long ago.
Grandmas are for caring
   about all the things you know.
Grandmas are for rocking you
   and singing you to sleep.
Grandmas are for giving you
   nice memories to keep.
Grandmas are for knowing
   all the things you're dreaming of.
But, most importantly of all,
   grandmas are for love.

AUTHOR UNKNOWN

INTRODUCTION

Being a grandmother is one of the greatest joys imaginable in life. But it takes more than genetics to become that truly Special Someone: *a grandma*. It takes wisdom, encouragement, forgiveness, comfort—and most of all, unconditional love.

The Best Grandma in the World celebrates the joy of grandmas everywhere, but most especially, it honors you, the unique and special grandma in my own heart. I hope this book inspires, encourages, and shows my appreciation to you, Grandma. I'm so honored and thankful that God has placed you in my life.

Grandma, you're the best!

You're the

BEST

GRANDMA

in the World Because...

You Take Time

to Listen.

If nothing is going well,

call your grandmother.

ITALIAN PROVERB

10

God has surely listened and heard my voice in prayer.

PSALM 66:19

You could probably listen to your grandchildren for hours on end and not wish for them to stop talking to you. The particular ways in which they phrase things and the fact that they're sharing their hearts with you make each moment precious, and you hang on every word. A phone call from a grandchild, no matter what time of day, is never a disturbance, but rather a welcome blessing.

We know that God is also available and willing to listen to us at any time, yet we sometimes need to be reminded of how much pleasure He takes in these conversations. Just as one of your grandchildren climbing up in your lap to tell you about his day makes you feel loved and valuable, your prayers express to God your love for and trust in Him. So take some time today to sit in your Father's lap and share with Him your hopes, dreams, cares—anything that's on your mind. He loves spending time with His children.

A LETTER TO MY GRANDMA

Dear Grandma,

You have always been there for me with a listening ear and an open heart. You know just what to say to make me feel better. Sometimes you share a story with me about your life, and other times, you have a wise word of advice or encouragement. You're also sensitive to when I just need someone to listen as I work things out on my own. You are more than a family member—you are my friend in whom I know I can always confide.

Thank you, Grandma, for your willingness to listen and your caring, gentle way. I want to follow in your footsteps so I may be a friend and confidante to those I love.

Love,

Your Grandchild

GRANDMA

I really feel quite special
That God has chosen you,
To be a person in my life
Who knows me through and through.

The time that we spend talking
I've always felt you heard . . .
You've been so good at listening
To each and every word.

And even things I didn't share,
You somehow heard them too.
I think this is a special gift
That God has given you.

So I just want to thank you
For being there for me,
And showing me acceptance
And love so totally.

AUTHOR UNKNOWN

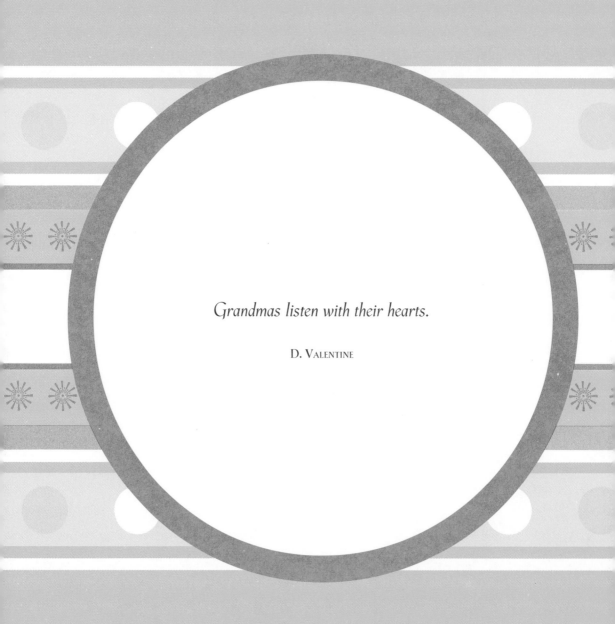

Grandmas listen with their hearts.

D. Valentine

MOST BEAUTIFULEST OF ALL

By Sally Clark

When I was five years old, I loved kindergarten, most of the time. But one day when it was raining, my grandma picked me up and my face must have looked like the drizzle falling all around us.

"What's the matter, baby?" Grandma asked me as I climbed into the car. "Did you have a bad day?"

"Don't ask me about that, Grandma. I don't want to talk about it!" I thundered. "You always ask me that! Don't ask me anymore!" I scowled and tried to turn away so she couldn't see my face.

"I see," said Grandma as she drove away from the school, and she didn't ask me anything else.

While the lightning flashed all around our car, I exploded, "My daddy says that I'm the most beautiful little girl in the whole world! No one is more beautifuler than me, not even Hannah. Hannah's daddy said that she's the most beautifulest little girl in the whole world, but he's wrong!"

"Well," Grandma said, "all daddies think that their little girls are the most beautiful little girls in the whole world because they love them so much. You and Hannah are both beautiful little girls, and both your daddies love you."

That was not what I wanted to hear. Wasn't Grandma on my side? When we got to the house, we sat in her car, waiting for the rain to stop, and Grandma tried to talk to me some more. I hung my head so she couldn't see that my eyes were beginning to puddle.

"Honey, why is it so important to you to be the most beautiful?" Grandma asked.

I didn't want to answer her. I didn't want to admit the truth. I hugged my door handle and picked at something I thought I saw there.

Grandma reached across the seat to touch my arm and said again, "Why is it so important to you to be more beautiful than Hannah? What happened today when you and Hannah were playing at school?"

I finally answered softly, "When I was talking to Hannah on the playground, she just turned away from me. I didn't even get to finish what I was saying. That's because Hannah is more beautifuler than me." Two big teardrops fell into my lap.

After a few moments, Grandma said, "I know how that feels. People do that to me sometimes, too, and I just hate it! It always makes me feel like I'm not as important as they are."

I raised my head, surprised that Grandma understood how I felt. Climbing across the car to the shelter of her lap, we listened to the rain splash against the windshield.

Grandma whispered, "You are always important to me, Sally, and you are always important to God. And no little girl is more beautiful than the one who believes God loves her."

I now walk in the beauty of knowing God loves me every day—because my grandma listened . . . and cared.[1]

Grandmas always say,
"Tell me more."

R. NORTON

※ ※ ※ ※ ※

Heavenly Father,

I love to listen to what my grandchildren have to say. When they confide in me about something that is troubling them or trust me with a secret, it makes me feel honored and reminds me of the important role I play in their lives.

Thank You for feeling the same way about me. You're always there to listen whenever I need someone to talk to. You've carried me through many lonely moments in my life, and it's always comforting to know that I can take my most secret thoughts to You with no fear of being criticized or rejected for them.

Help my grandchildren to know that not only am I there for them anytime they need someone to talk to, but that You are there for them as well. While I love being the one they come to with their secrets, I want nothing more than to see each of them enjoy a personal relationship with You.

Amen.

I THANK GOD for you, GRANDMA.

You always LISTEN to me!

You're the

BEST

GRANDMA

in the World Because...

You Share Your

Wisdom.

It's easier to have the vigor of youth

when you're old than the

wisdom of age when you're young.

RICHARD J. NEEDHAM

*[A woman of noble character] speaks with wisdom,
and faithful instruction is on her tongue.*

PROVERBS 31:26

You've learned a great deal through your experiences in life, both the good times and the not so good. You want to share what you've learned with those you love the most because it pains you to see them make any of the same mistakes you've made or get into situations you know would be best for them to avoid. Yet, sometimes it's difficult to know when to speak up and also when to hold your tongue and let your loved one do the talking.

You should always be sure that your sharing of advice is motivated by love and that you are following the Holy Spirit's leading. But don't be too quick to shy away from an opportunity to share your wisdom with the people you love. The wisdom you've gained along your life's journey is a gift from God, and it's meant to be shared with your family. And, as a grandma, you have a unique opportunity to relate sound advice to your grandchildren, who may look up to you greatly. They need the valuable wisdom God wants to communicate to them through you.

A LETTER TO MY GRANDMA

Dear Grandma,

You've always been the quiet, gentle type. At family get-togethers, you usually go about your business silently, content to let others do most of the talking. When you do speak up, your words are laced with wisdom—presented in your humble, sweet way yet so profound. When I take the time to sit down with you and really get you talking, I find a treasury of wisdom compiled from your years of experiences, both common and exciting. I always walk away from these precious conversations having learned something new, not only about you, but also about life and about myself.

Thank you, Grandma, for the wisdom you've shared with me and for the meek, humble way in which you present it. I want to learn all I can from you in the time we have together.

Love,

Your Grandchild

A grandmother's

wisdom is a

priceless treasure—

worth more than

pure gold.

AUTHOR UNKNOWN

Wisdom is knowledge tempered with judgment.

LORD RITCHIE-CALDER

GRANDMA'S MICROWAVE

By Robert Wall

My grandmother had always shunned gadgets and other sorts of kitchen technology. Having learned to cook in the 1920s, she stuck to the "old standbys"—a good toaster, an antiquated hand mixer, and a no-nonsense blender. Her pots and pans were probably thirty years old, but her kitchen produced quite possibly the best food I've ever tasted.

Some time during my teen years, my mother and her siblings determined that Grandma needed a microwave. "It will help her out so much," they reasoned. "She can microwave leftovers. And don't forget water for tea! It will save her so much time." Firmly convinced, they all pitched in at Christmas and bought her a shiny new microwave.

The microwave was installed with much fanfare. Several of my mother's siblings descended on Grandma's kitchen, moved some exposed stacks of baking pans onto an upper shelf, and proudly placed the microwave on the counter where the pans had been. Beaming proudly, they explained to Grandma both how to operate the microwave and how much time it would save her. A dubious Grandma reluctantly nodded, and they left.

I had the opportunity to spend the night at my grandmother's house the following February. Looking for a snack in the middle of the afternoon, I tossed some leftovers into a bowl (Grandma's leftovers were always the best) and headed for the microwave.

Guess what I saw when I opened the microwave. Pans! Yes, the very same pans that had been moved off the counter to clear space for the microwave. As Grandma strolled into the kitchen, I had to know . . . why did she keep her metal pans in the microwave? She smiled, and replied, "Oh, I only use the microwave about once every two months. When you use it, you have to stir things, flip them over, rotate them . . . it just takes too much time."

Too much time? I wondered to myself. I was curious.

The next morning, I watched carefully. She shaped two handfuls of leftover mashed potatoes into patties, and a couple of breakfast sausages joined them in an old pie tin. Into the oven it went. Putting a tea kettle on to boil, Grandma went to do her hair.

After she finished her hair, out came the potatoes and sausage, and off came the teakettle. She dumped two packets of cocoa into mugs, poured the hot water, divided the potatoes and sausage, and breakfast was served. She just couldn't be bothered waiting for something that wasted as much time as the microwave!

Isn't it ironic that we spend so much effort trying to save time, and so little effort actually enjoying the time we have? I don't recall ever seeing Grandma run. If I had, I would have assumed that the house was on fire. She was never in a hurry. She wasn't stressed about "saving time," yet she always seemed to have plenty of it.

The memory of that microwave, wedged full of baking pans, still makes me smile. Of all the things Grandma taught me, this lesson sticks with me the most: It's not "saving time" that matters, but spending it well.[2]

The most manifest sign of wisdom
is continued cheerfulness.

MONTAIGNE

Heavenly Father,

Thank You for Your great wisdom that You've shared with us in Your Word, the Bible. Through it, You've directed my steps and made my life much richer and more meaningful than it would have been had I just relied on my own knowledge to get me through. You've helped me to avoid painful mistakes and to experience the joy of living according to Your plan.

Please help my loved ones to see and experience for themselves the value of living according to Your Word. May my children look back with fondness at the times we spent together reading and studying the Bible as a family and pass that precious gift along to their children. When my grandchildren are with me, help me to lovingly direct them toward You in my words and actions. When they come to me for advice, give me the right words of wisdom and the Scripture they need at that moment. Help me to know how to pray with them. I want, more than anything, for them to be able to experience Your love through our time together.

Amen.

I THANK GOD for you,

my WISE Grandma!

You're the

BEST

GRANDMA

in the World Because...

You Make the
Ordinary Special.

Perfect love sometimes does not come

till the first grandchild.

Welsh Proverb

When I consider your heavens, the work of your fingers...what is man that you are mindful of him, the son of man that you care for him?

PSALM 8:3–4

Grandmas have a knack for detail. Whether they're picking out a present or baking cookies, their attention to the small things makes everything they do more special.

Margaret had an acute sense of detail that was most apparent in her love of nature. When her grandchildren visited, she enjoyed taking them on nature hikes in the mountains near her home. Although surrounded by towering peaks, the thing that was sure to catch Margaret's attention was the intricate marking on the tiniest wildflower growing along the path. She used examples like this to show them God's attention to detail which reveals His love.

Just as you put great care and attention into expressing your love to your grandchildren, your Heavenly Father has surrounded you with expressions of His love. Give thanks to Him for His marvelous care. Then pass that grateful attitude along to your grandchildren, helping them to recognize God's love for them.

A LETTER TO MY GRANDMA

Dear Grandma,

Every day I spend at your house is a special occasion. I can always count on waking up to some sort of special treat for breakfast—doughnuts with sprinkles that you went out early to pick up just for me, or muffins or pancakes that we make together. Sometimes we do crafts together or work in your garden. Other times, we go swimming or to the store to pick out a special toy. You and I must have a lot in common, because we always do the things I enjoy most in the world, and they seem to be the exact things you most like doing too. You make every day we're together a celebration, and you never miss a chance to make me feel loved and special.

Thank you, Grandma, for being so thoughtful. You bless my life in so many ways.

Love,

Your Grandchild

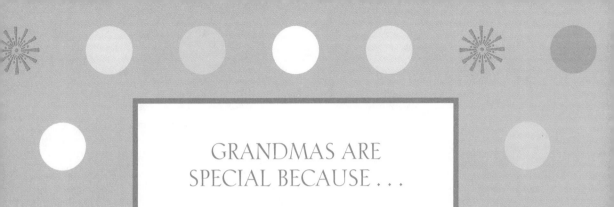

GRANDMAS ARE SPECIAL BECAUSE . . .

- They read my favorite books again and again and again.

- They talk to God about me.

- They visit my school.

- They let me make a mess in the kitchen.

- They know how to make tuna casserole from cans, not a box.

- They sit down at the table to eat dinner.

- They teach me manners and tell me I'll need them later.

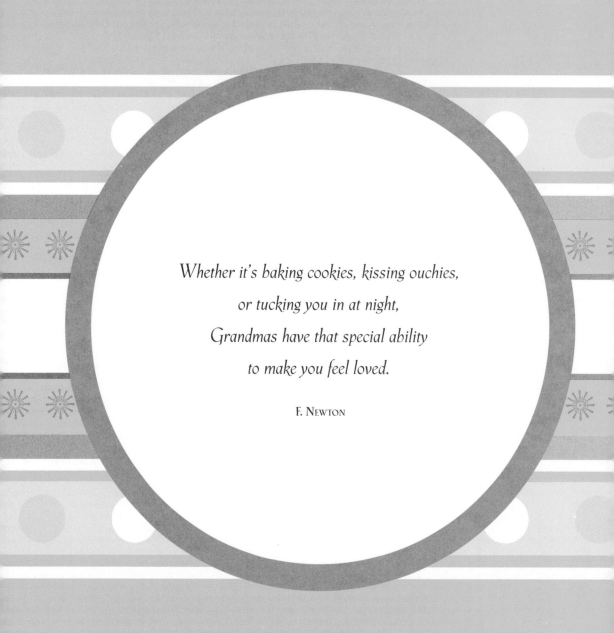

Whether it's baking cookies, kissing ouchies,

or tucking you in at night,

Grandmas have that special ability

to make you feel loved.

F. NEWTON

TASTES OF HOME

By Jeremy Moore

The taste of instant iced tea.

I was probably too young to drink it. Everyone told me that coffee would stunt my growth, and tea is just coffee for the stuffy man.

But I remember, every day at Grandma's house, there was cold, instant iced tea in a lime-green plastic, half-gallon jug.

And there was always enough for everyone.

Growing up next door to your grandparents is a kid's dream come true.

Our parents love us, but they are responsible for us. They have to make sure we grow up to become men and women, so sometimes they have to say no.

Grandparents get to say yes.

At home, the television had to stay off. Too much television rots your brain, our parents would say.

At Grandma's house, the television was always on, and it always had cartoons.

At home, we had homework.

At Grandma's house, we played outside. There was a swing set in Grandma's backyard made of steel and wood, not plastic.

In the old attic in Grandma's house, she and Grandpa had built a kids' play area that only we could fit into. It was our secret place, where we could plan and plot with our oversized imaginations.

In Grandma's living room, we would take all the cushions from the sofas and chairs and make a fort. When it was time to go home, our fort would stay. When we came back it was gone, but Grandma didn't seem to mind when we built it again.

Grandma had a model ship in a glass container. I wanted to touch it, so I lifted the glass. The glass broke, but the ship stayed on the shelf. Eventually it got dusty and she threw it away. I never saw her throw it away, and she never mentioned it.

Grandma used to take us to the library in her big car. She let me check out as many books as I wanted. She told me that as long as I loved to read, I would never be lonely and I would never be bored.

Grandma's house was always open. Grandma was always there with a hug, a smile, and a listening ear.

And a cold glass of instant iced tea.

I'm older now. I have children of my own. My parents have become grandparents.

I still have not gotten the taste of cold, instant iced tea quite right.

But I have learned the word *hospitality* and how much work goes into being hospitable.

That's what my grandmother was.

Hospitable.

But to me, it just felt like home.[3]

Grandmothers are the

wellspring that brings forth

our deepest feelings of love.

PHILLIP E. WAINWRIGHT

WHY I'M THANKFUL YOU'RE MY GRANDMA . . .

- You like to take naps as much as I do!

- You always have food in your purse.

- You cheer for me at ball games.

- You worry about me and call just to check up on me.

- You don't mind taking me to the store.

- You love to buy things for me.

Grandmas are God's gift to children.

AUTHOR UNKNOWN

✻ ✻ ✻ ✻ ✻

Lord,

Grandchildren are such a blessing. I thank You for each one of mine. I have such fun with them when we're together. Listening to their laughter and seeing their bright, hopeful smiles bring joy to my heart and make me feel young again.

It's nice to finally have the time to do with them some of the things I wasn't always able to do with my children. I love to have them sit in my lap as I read them a story or listen to what's happening in their lives. It's exciting to spend time with them outside, experiencing the wonder of Your creation through their eyes. And I especially enjoy doing little things to make our time together memorable. Whether it's fixing a special breakfast or doing a craft or baking with them or surprising them with a special treat on their pillows at bedtime—it thrills my heart to bless them with these small gifts.

Thank You for the gift of grandchildren and for the infectious joy they bring to my life.

Amen.

I THANK GOD for you, GRANDMA.

Everything's SPECIAL when you're around!

You're the
BEST
GRANDMA
in the World Because...

You Love Me Even
When I Mess Up.

Grandmas have a short memory when it comes to their grandkids' shortcomings.

D. VALENTINE

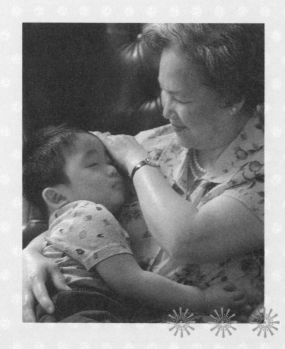

In [Christ] we have redemption through his blood, the forgiveness of sins, in accordance with the riches of God's grace that he lavished on us.

EPHESIANS 1:7–8

Grandparents have an uncanny ability to see only the good in their grandchildren. Even though they see weaknesses in their grandchildren, they choose to focus instead on their strengths.

Our Heavenly Father sees us in much the same way. When we ask forgiveness for our sins, God completely erases them from His memory. Because we are covered by Jesus' blood through the sacrifice He made on our behalf, the Father sees us as perfect, holy, and righteous.

The psalmist David describes God's forgiveness in this way: "As far as the east is from the west, so far has he removed our transgressions from us" (Psalm 103:12). The author of Hebrews says that through Jesus' one sacrifice, "he has made perfect forever those who are being made holy" (Hebrews 10:14). Isn't it comforting to know that you are as perfect in God's eyes as that precious grandchild who cuddles up in your lap?

A LETTER TO MY GRANDMA

Dear Grandma,

All my life, when I've done something I knew I shouldn't have, the person it's been hardest to confess to is you—not because you make it hard, but because I never want to disappoint you. Yet I always end up confiding in you, and it feels so good when I do because I know I can count on you to immediately forgive me. Our relationship is never hurt by what I've done. Instead, you let me know each time how much you love me and what an amazing person you think I am.

Though I haven't always known it at the time, you've been teaching me about God's love and forgiveness through each of these experiences. Because I've always been able to confide in you, it's easier for me now to go to God and confess my wrongdoings, knowing that our relationship won't be hurt and that He'll accept me with the same love and forgiveness that you have all these years. Thank you, Grandma, for your wonderful example of unconditional love.

Love,

Your Grandchild

I once cried in my

grandmother's arms,

and with her embrace

she made the world

right again.

PHILLIP E. WAINWRIGHT

Forgiveness is a funny thing. It warms

the heart and cools the sting.

WILLIAM ARTHUR WARD

IF IT'S TUESDAY

By Alice Malloy

From the kitchen I hear the crash and the baby's wail. "Oh, my gosh!" I shout as I reach the scene in the living room. The bouncer is upended, baby and all, and her two-year-old brother stands beside it, wide-eyed, lips quivering. I pull the baby into my arms and check her body for welts and bruises. All clear. Hugs and kisses calm her, and I turn my attention to the culprit, who stretches his arms upward.

"Up," he cries. His eyes fill with tears. "Up."

I sweep him into my free arm. "It's all right, lovey," I say between kisses. "You have to be gentle with baby sister; you could hurt her."

It is Grandma day at my house, and I'm hoping my grandson's rambunctious activity is a result of Easter candy and not his recent second birthday.

I am not the kind of grandparent I intended to be. After raising five children, I planned to model this phase of life after my mother, who defined her grandmotherly intentions days after my first child was born. "I will not babysit. In fact, I'll be happy to hire a babysitter for you, but I will not babysit."

There was no doubt my mother loved the children, and they loved her, but all were content to sit across the table from one another sipping tea and eating oatmeal cookies for an hour twice a week. There was no diaper changing, lap sitting, or neck nuzzling in my mother's house. Just short, polite visits and occasional dinners, always with me in attendance, the keys to the car in my pocket in case someone forgot the rules.

It worked for my mother, and I imagined it working for me. But when my son placed my first grandchild in my arms, I fell in love. Defenses melted, and the hardness in me turned to mush.

"Do I have to give him back?" I asked.

My waking hours following the birth of this baby were filled with a long-ing like one feels for a new love. Dropping by for baby hugs became part of my daily routine. It was a gift to hold this new little life close and breathe in his newness, to watch his face when he slept and his eyes wander around the room when he was awake. I couldn't get enough of him.

And so when it was time for my daughter-in-law to return to work, I found myself offering to babysit one day a week.

"Are you sure?"

I wasn't really, and I thought of telling them I'd changed my mind. *What are you thinking?* I asked myself. *This is your time. You've raised your children, cut back on work. You're free. You have time to write, read, do whatever you want. Don't you remember how old you are?*

"I'll give it a try," I told my son and his wife. "We'll see how it goes, whether it's too much."

That was the beginning of our Tuesdays together. They belonged to little Gordie and me. Everything else was put aside—appointments, phone calls, bills. I fed, diapered, and cooed. I reveled in his smiles and tickled him into giggles. We played peek-a-boo and so-big and read *Goodnight Moon.* I searched his gums for budding teeth and watched as he took his first wobbly steps between the couch and coffee table, applauding himself when he reached his goal. We went to the beach and threw rocks in the water and went "so high" on the swings in the park. We stopped at the bakery and ate cookies before lunch. I heard his first words. And then words formed sentences.

The mother/disciplinarian in me from years ago no longer exists. I stand by calmly as he empties the ice tray in my refrigerator or the bowls from a kitchen cabinet. I get down on my knees with him to wipe up the water he spills from the cooler. Cheerios on the floor, a broken dish are no problem. I don't scold. I am Grandma.

Now there is a little sister who joins us on Tuesdays. Caitlin is a chubby baby who spends her days eating, sleeping, and smiling. She is the promise of more firsts.

So every Tuesday my son pulls his SUV into my driveway and unloads babies and bags of diapers, clothes, and bottles. A little boy strolls up my walk, smiles, and holds out his arms for me to pick him up. Behind him is his father carrying an infant seat overflowing with a baby girl. Her eyes crinkle in recognition when she sees me.

"Anytime you feel it's too much, just let us know," he says.

Not a chance.[4]

Love is patient, love is kind. ... It keeps no record of wrongs.

1 Corinthians 13:4–5

✳ ✳ ✳ ✳ ✳

Heavenly Father,

It's difficult for me to believe that my grandchildren are even capable of doing anything wrong. They're so small and innocent; someone else must surely be to blame, right? Yet, when I'm honest with myself, I know that none of us are immune to our own human, sinful natures—even my "perfect" grandchildren.

When they make mistakes or decide to sway from the path of Your righteousness, help them to know the immeasurable vastness of Your forgiveness. May they be quick to come to You with repentant hearts. And when they do, may they experience the fullness of Your love for them.

I hope they will also know that they can come to me if they need a listening ear. I want them to feel safe confiding in me, knowing that I won't judge them or love them any less for what they've done. It's a great privilege to be able to share this kind of relationship with my grandchildren and know I can be there for them without having to be the disciplinarian.

Thank You for Your watchful care over my grandchildren.

Amen.

I THANK GOD for you,

my forgiving GRANDMA!

You're the

BEST

GRANDMA

in the World Because...

You Know

the Best Remedy for

My Hurts.

There is no illness that can't be made better

by a hug from Grandma!

CHARLOTTE MAE

Praise be to the God and Father of our Lord Jesus Christ,
the Father of compassion and the God of all comfort, who comforts
us in all our troubles, so that we can comfort those in any trouble
with the comfort we ourselves have received from God.

2 CORINTHIANS 1:3–4

God is great at comforting His hurting children. You've probably experienced many times over the unexplainable peace and assurance He can provide in the midst of the most hopeless-looking situation.

When your grandchildren confide in you and bring you their cares and hurts, you have the opportunity to share with them the comfort and peace that accompanies a personal relationship with God. Whether you're counseling a grandchild who is having serious problems at school or applying a bandage to a tiny paper cut, your careful concern demonstrates God's loving attentiveness to our needs.

And when you take your grandchildren's concerns to God in prayer, you are placing them in the most capable hands of all.

A LETTER TO MY GRANDMA

Dear Grandma,

You've always had the best shoulder for crying on. When I was small and scraped my knee riding my bike, you knew just how to dry my tears and always had a Band-Aid and a cup of chocolate milk on hand to ease my pain. When I suffered from a broken heart after a teenage romance came to an end, you let me pour out my heart to you, then told me about your first romance and its comical, "tragic" ending. Now that I'm older, I still find myself calling you when I've had a rough day or need someone to pray with me about something. You always seem to have a word of comfort or an interesting story to brighten my day.

Thank you, Grandma, for the comfort you've brought me and all those around you. If you ever need a shoulder to cry on, please know that I'm here for you.

Love,

Your Grandchild

When I scrape my knee,

Grandma's kisses are

better than a bandage!

R. NORTON

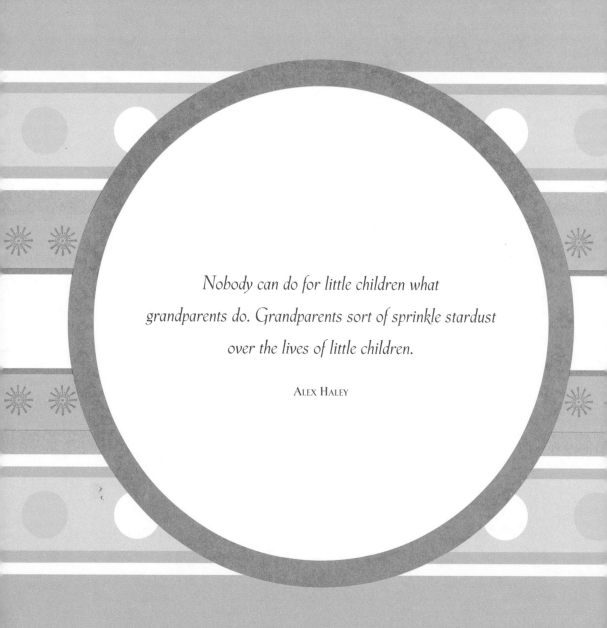

Nobody can do for little children what grandparents do. Grandparents sort of sprinkle stardust over the lives of little children.

ALEX HALEY

THE SINGING MAMAW

By Donna J. Shepherd

Brooke has the widest smile, the most sparkling eyes, and the sweetest voice of any grandchild in the world—according to her grandma, Shirley.

Even though five-year-old Brooke has SMA—Spinal Muscular Atrophy—and spends the better part of her day in a wheelchair, her cheerful attitude keeps those around her entertained. Behind the smile lies a bit of mischievousness. Sometimes her voice comes out whiny and cajoling, but when Brooke bats those long eyelashes and says, "Please," no one can turn down any request, and she knows it!

Because of Brooke's medical condition, her mom, Ginger, needs to fly her cross-country several times a year for tests. It's a difficult task to transport Brooke, her wheelchair, and her baby sister—who also happens to have SMA. That's where Grandma comes in.

In spite of the fact that she recently had surgery for carpal tunnel syndrome, Shirley lifts and tugs and carries the children anyplace they need to be. At the end of the day, with her wrists in braces, she takes a couple of anti-inflammatory pills and collapses into bed. Her rest doesn't last long.

A thin, high voice calls out from the nearby bed, "Mamaw, are you awake?"

Brooke doesn't have enough muscle tone to turn herself over. Shirley climbs out of bed to reposition her. She will do this several more times before the night is through.

In the morning light, Brooke gives her grandma an angelic smile, and says, "Mamaw, I counted, and I only had to get you up four times."

Shirley's eyes fill with tears. This child keeps track of the kindnesses she receives. "Honey, Mamaw would get up a hundred times if you needed me."

For a few of the tests, Brooke can be sedated, but one test requires that she remain alert. To take Brooke's mind off the discomfort, Shirley always sings to her during the test. When the time comes to be placed aboard the gurney and rolled down the hospital hallway for the dreaded test, Brooke calls out in a plaintive tone, "Mamaw, I need you to sing."

A nurse standing at her station speaks up and tells Shirley, "I notice that that baby's mom is standing right beside her, yet she calls for you. You must be the best grandma in the whole world."

Shirley looks at Brooke, so young and frail, who has to endure these tests time and again. The doctors have already told the family she may never walk, and in fact, may not live past her teens. Each moment spent with Brooke is precious, and every "Mamaw" sounds like the sweetest sound in the world.

Shirley turns to the nurse and says, "As a grandma, I may not be the best, but as Brooke's Mamaw, I'm the most blessed."

And then she takes Brooke's chubby hand into her aching one and begins to sing.[5] ✳ ✳ ✳ ✳ ✳

Grandmas never run out

of the two most

important things in life:

hugs and cookies.

AUTHOR UNKNOWN

GRANDMA'S HUGS
ARE MADE OF LOVE

Everything my grandma does
Is something special made with love.
She takes time to add the extra touch
That says, "I love you very much."

She fixes hurts with a kiss and smile
And tells good stories grandma-style.
It's warm and cozy on her lap
For secret-telling or a nap.

And when I say my prayer at night,
I ask God to bless and hold her tight.
'Cause when it comes to giving hugs
My grandma's arms are filled with love.

AUTHOR UNKNOWN

Grandma's house is like a little corner of heaven—
full of unconditional love.

AUTHOR UNKNOWN

✳ ✳ ✳ ✳ ✳

Lord,

When my grandchildren are hurting, it hurts me too. They seem so young and fragile to me, and it feels unfair at times that they should experience any kind of pain. Yet, I know that disappointments and hurts are a natural part of life in a fallen world and that You are able to bring good out of any situation, strengthening their relationship with You even in the midst of hardships.

Whether their hurts are great or small, help me to provide the comfort and understanding they need. Help me also to point them toward You as the ultimate source of strength and comfort. May they learn to rely on Your capable arms to carry them through life's difficult moments.

Thank You for those precious moments I'm able to spend with them in prayer. I don't want to miss even one opportunity to share with them my great Comforter, Friend, and the Lover of my soul and theirs.

Amen.

I THANK GOD for you, GRANDMA.

You know how to make EVERYTHING better!

You're the

BEST

GRANDMA

in the World Because…

You Think of

Everything.

Grandmother—

a wonderful mother with

lots of practice.

AUTHOR UNKNOWN

God is able to make all grace abound to you,
so that in all things at all times, having all that you need,
you will abound in every good work.

2 CORINTHIANS 9:8

Just as you love to do thoughtful things for your friends and family, God loves to do thoughtful things for His children. And He does—every day. He's provided you with everything you've needed in order to become the person you are today. He's given you unique talents that have equipped you to be a wonderful mother and grandmother. He's supplied you with the time and resources you've needed to do what He's called you to do. And He continues to bless you with new energy, ideas, resources, and inspiration.

As you talk with your Heavenly Father today, take a moment to reflect on His thoughtfulness toward you. Thank Him for supplying all of your needs and for the many unique and creative ways in which He's blessed your life.

A LETTER TO MY GRANDMA

Dear Grandma,

As a child, when I came to visit you, there were certain things that could be depended upon. There would always be special treats in the kitchen cabinets carefully selected just for me. The beds would be carefully made and turned down at night, and everything would be neatly in place without a speck of dust in sight. A homemade lunch would be on the table promptly at noon, dinner at five o'clock. When Sunday morning came, we would go to church to worship together. And there was always plenty of time for playing the piano, reading a good book, or taking a walk around the neighborhood. You taught me how to slow down a bit and to capture all of life's joys, even the small ones that often go unnoticed.

I'll always cherish those special times with you, Grandma. Thank you for your love that has always been as constant and thoughtful as the memories you've created for me.

Love,

Your Grandchild

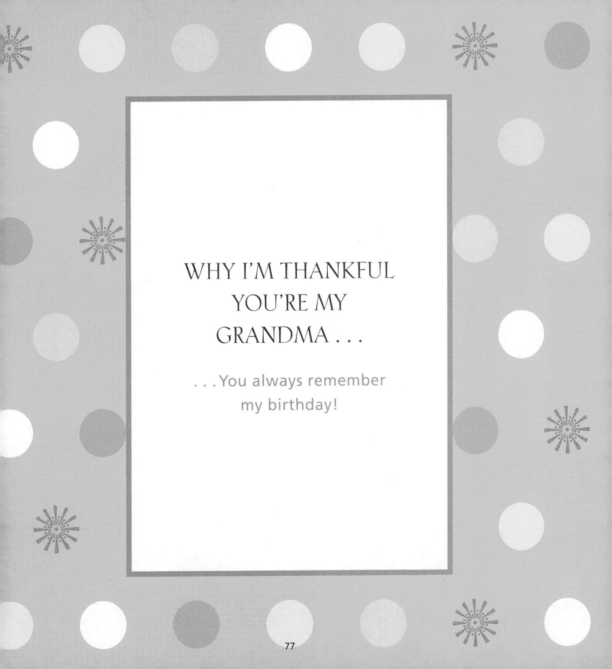

WHY I'M THANKFUL YOU'RE MY GRANDMA . . .

. . . You always remember
my birthday!

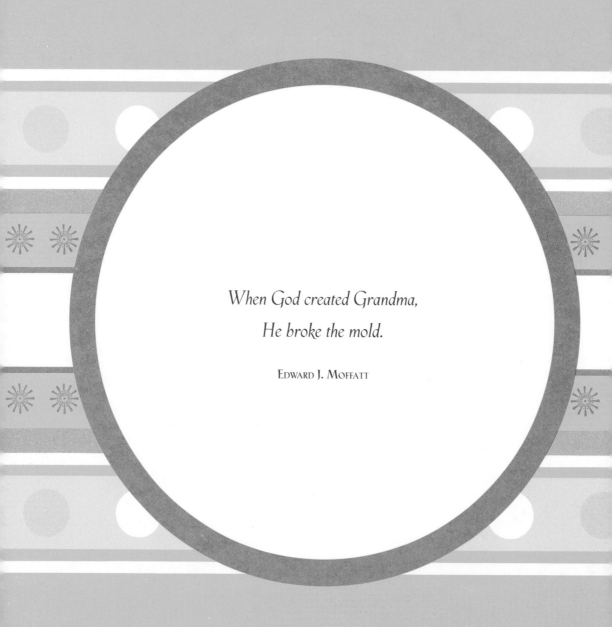

When God created Grandma,

He broke the mold.

EDWARD J. MOFFATT

A GRANDMA'S GIFT OF THE HEART ✳ ✳ ✳ ✳ ✳

By Renie Burghardt

My eleventh birthday was a week away when we arrived at the refugee camp in Austria on that cold November day in 1947. My grandparents and I had fled our Soviet-occupied country of Hungary with only the clothes on our backs.

To frightened, cold, and hungry people like us, the displaced-persons camp was a blessing from God. We were given our own little cardboard-enclosed cubicle in a barrack, fed hot soup, and supplied with warm clothes. We had much to be grateful for. But as for my upcoming birthday, I didn't even want to think about it. We had left Hungary without possessions or money, but we were still alive. That was the important thing. So I put birthday presents and celebrations behind me.

My grandmother was the only mother I had ever known because her only child, my mother, had died suddenly when I was just a few weeks old. Before World War II intensified, my birthdays had been grand celebrations with many cousins in attendance and lots of gifts.

My eighth birthday had been the last time I received a store-bought gift. Times were already hard then, money was scarce, and survival was our utmost goal. But Grandma had managed to pawn something so she could buy me a book. I loved it!

Cilike's Adventures, a wonderful book full of humor and adventure, had transported me many times from the harshness of the real world to a world of laughter and fun.

On November 25, when I awoke in our cardboard cubicle, I laid there and thought about being eleven. I was practically a grown-up, I told myself, and I would act accordingly when my grandparents awoke. I didn't want them to feel bad because they couldn't give me a present. So I dressed quickly and tiptoed out as quietly as possible. I ran across the frosty dirt road to the barrack marked "Women's Bathroom and Shower," washed, combed my hair, and finally returned to our cardboard sleeping quarters.

"Good morning, sweetheart! Happy birthday," Grandpa greeted me cheerily.

"Thank you, but I'd just as soon forget about birthdays from now on." I squirmed in his generous hug.

"You are too young to forget about birthdays," Grandma said. "Besides, who would I give this present to if birthdays are to be forgotten?"

"Present?" I looked at her in surprise as she reached into her pocket and pulled something out.

"Happy birthday, sweetheart. It's not much of a present, but I thought you might like having Cilike back on your eleventh birthday," she said, tears welling up in her eyes.

"My old Cilike book! But I thought we left it behind," I said. I hugged the book to my chest while tears of joy flowed down my cheeks.

"Well, we almost did," Grandma said. "But when we had to leave so quickly in the middle of the night, I grabbed it, along with my prayer book, and stuck it in my pocket. I knew how much you loved that book, so I couldn't bear to leave it behind. I'm sorry it's not a new book, but I hope you like having it back."

"Oh, thank you, Grandma! Having Cilike back means so much to me. So very much." I hugged her again. "It's the best birthday present I ever received!"

The gift of that old book was a miracle to me, and I realized that day that God had blessed me with a wonderful grandmother, whose love would always see me through the hard times. And most importantly, she taught me that gifts of the heart are always the best gifts, because they truly are gifts of love.[6]

The best things you can give children,
next to good habits, are good memories.

SYDNEY J. HARRIS

✳ ✳ ✳ ✳ ✳

Heavenly Father,

One of my greatest joys in life is being able to do special things for my grandchildren. When one of my grandchildren opens a present from me, it thrills my heart to hear, "Grandma, you remembered!" or "How did you know, Grandma? It's just what I've always wanted!"

Though it's not always easy, I feel like it's important for me to keep up with what makes each of my grandchildren unique—their likes, dislikes, special interests, talents, and personalities. Though I love them all equally, I never want to treat them like they're all alike. Instead I want to make sure they know that I recognize them as individuals. I want them to feel known and loved for who they are deep down inside.

Help my mind to stay sharp and keen so I can continue to do thoughtful things for my family. Give me fresh inspiration for ways to make them feel special, loved, and appreciated.

Amen.

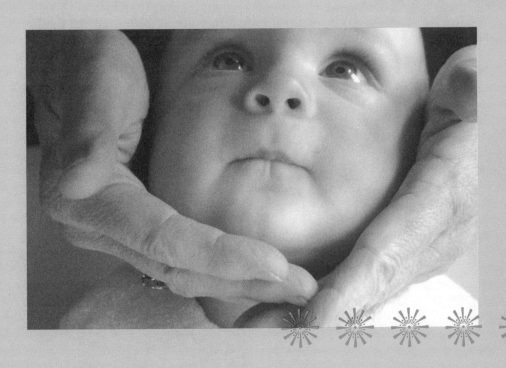

I THANK GOD for you, GRANDMA.

You always THINK of me!

You're the

BEST

GRANDMA

in the World Because...

You Make Me Feel

Like a Star.

When I walk into the room,

Grandma's eyes always light up.

She makes me feel like I'm the

most special person in the world.

PRISCILLA COTTON

From the lips of children and infants you have ordained praise.

PSALM 8:2

It probably comes quite naturally for you to heap praises upon your grandchildren. It's fun to watch their progress in school or to be a part of their special activities, and they can always count on Grandma for a word of praise or a special treat for a job well done.

Is it equally easy to heap praises upon your Heavenly Father? If so, pass this spirit of praise and thanksgiving along to your grandchildren. Share with them your favorite hymns or other worship music. If you play an instrument, play songs of praise around your grandchildren and encourage them to sing along. They would probably also love for you to teach them how to play a simple tune.

What a valuable gift you bestow on your grandchildren when you teach them of the joy found in giving praise to God. After all, worship is one of the primary purposes for which they were created, and they'll find their greatest fulfillment in living lives of praise.

A LETTER TO MY GRANDMA

Dear Grandma,

I remember you taking me out with you sometimes and introducing me to a few of your friends. These times always gave me a huge boost of confidence. When you'd introduce me, your eyes would glisten with pride. You would quickly pull out pictures of me from my latest ball game or special event and tell your friends all about my recent accomplishments. I may have been a cloud with no speaking part in the school play, but according to you, I stole the show. And those two minutes I got to play in the basketball game, rather than warming the bench, were the most crucial—the team simply couldn't have won without me. At least that's how you told it.

Thank you, Grandma, for your confidence in me. Because of you, I've learned to believe in myself and have accomplished things I never would have thought possible except for the fact that my grandma just knew I would succeed.

Love,

Your Grandchild

When we play
hide-and-seek,
Grandma always pretends
she can't find me.

AUTHOR UNKNOWN

It is as grandmothers that our mothers

come into the fullness of their grace.

FINDING THE LIGHT

By Carrie Younce

It's the little things that made the biggest difference.

My grandma—the woman who stood on her feet for up to ten hours a day at a manual cash register in the local grocery—always made time for me. She always had mints in her purse just for me. Grandma always made me feel as if she really wanted me around.

When I got to spend the night with her that one weekend a month, I felt as if I were a queen. I got to help plan the menu and set the table. I got to choose the games to play with her and Grandpa after dinner.

Grandma taught me how to beat her at cards, namely Old Maid, Go Fish, and Crazy Eights. She taught me how to cook perfectly crispy bacon for BLT sandwiches, how to mash the potatoes so that the lumps were mostly gone, how to loop rag-string pot holders, and how to make modeling clay castles. And she taught me how not to be afraid of the dark.

When it was time for bed (with Grandpa on temporary vacation in their guest room), I piled into the king-sized bed with a nest of pillows and my grandma. Then she switched off the light, throwing the room into an inky, pitch-black darkness.

I turned my face into my pillow, whimpering softly, but just loud enough to be heard. "What's wrong, Sweetie?" Grandma's voice reached out in the darkness to soothe me.

"I'm scared."

"Why are you scared?"

"It's dark."

"Honey, there's nothing there in the dark that wasn't there in the light. Here," she said as she slid over and pulled me into her arms. "I'll show you it's not as dark as you think it is. Close your eyes really, really tight and keep them closed while I count to ten."

I trustingly closed my eyes, knowing that she was doing it, too, as she counted slowly to ten.

"Now, open your eyes," she whispered.

I opened my eyes and I could see it. I could see the light from the ever-present stars and moon as they framed the window shade just brightly enough to see the outlines of all the familiar items in her room.

"See?" She kissed my temple and smoothed back my hair. "The light is always there. You just have to know how to find it."

I found the light, and years later, when my daughter cried out in the night, I showed her how not to be afraid.

Pulling her up into my lap, I spoke the words from a memory I had tucked away in a dusty corner of my mind.

"Close your eyes really, really tight and count to ten . . ."

Incredible warmth welled up in my heart as I shared with my child what my grandma had given to me—the truth that darkness can never fully extinguish the light. The light is always there. We just have to remember how to find it.[7]

A grandmother is

a little bit parent,

a little bit teacher,

and a little bit best friend.

AUTHOR UNKNOWN

GRANDMA ALWAYS
MAKES ME FEEL SO GOOD

She thinks I'm smarter than I really am.

She laughs at my knock-knock jokes.

She tells me funny stories of when she was little.

She sits down with me to talk.

She thinks I'm clever.

She shows off pictures of me.

She buys me things that Mom says are too expensive.

She has an endless supply of kisses.

No cowboy was ever faster on the draw
than a grandma pulling a baby picture out of her purse.

AUTHOR UNKNOWN

✳ ✳ ✳ ✳ ✳

Lord,

I never feel so loved, appreciated, and adored as when I'm in the presence of my grandchildren. They have a way about them of making me feel like the queen of their little world. A simple "I love you, Grandma!" or "Grandma, you're the best!" can make my heart swell and carry me through the most trying day.

Father, this is just one of the many ways You provide for my specific needs. With a whole universe to orchestrate, You find the time to place into my life just the right person with the appropriate word of encouragement at the very moment I need it most. Your loving care for me is overwhelming.

Thank You for the love and admiration of my grandchildren, these precious blessings You've given me. May each of them know how special they are to me and what a difference they make in my life.

Amen.

I THANK GOD for you, GRANDMA.

You always make me feel SPECIAL!

You're the

BEST
GRANDMA
in the World Because...

You Encourage Me

to Follow

My Dreams.

What do we teach

our children? We should

say to each of them:

Do you know what you are?

You are a marvel.

You are unique! You may

become a Shakespeare, a

Michelangelo, a Beethoven.

You have the capacity

for anything.

PABLO CASALS

Do not let any unwholesome talk come out of your mouths, but only what is helpful for building others up according to their needs, that it may benefit those who listen.

EPHESIANS 4:29

What amazing encouragers Grandmas are! Because they truly believe their grandchildren are the very best at whatever they do, Grandmas have a way of instilling confidence and inspiring dreams within the hearts of their grandchildren.

You do not know what dream may be sparked by your simple words of praise. One of your grandchildren may become a famous artist because you loved her childhood drawings and proudly displayed them. Another may minister to hundreds as a missionary because you recognized his heart of compassion. Still another may save many lives as a doctor because of your praise of her excellent grades in science.

All of your grandchildren will benefit greatly from your faithful prayers about their futures, your words of advice and encouragement, and your faithful support of their dreams.

A LETTER TO MY GRANDMA

Dear Grandma,

I've always loved taking walks with you. It's during these times that I feel I can open up to you and tell you about all the dreams and plans that are on my heart. You listen attentively, then tell me about some of the dreams you've had along your life's journey. Some of them have become realities, and some have not, but you always tell me you're better off for having followed your dreams, even when they've taken you in an unexpected direction. You encourage me to dream big and to act on those dreams, and you never laugh at my ideas or think them juvenile or far-fetched.

I treasure those special moments with you, Grandma, when it's just the two of us. I hope you know how much your encouragement means to me. You've made such a difference in my life.

Love,

Your Grandchild

Grandmas are

eternal encouragers.

They inspire us to

follow our dreams.

VALENCIA SMITH

Praise the young and they will make progress.

IRISH PROVERB

LESSON IN THE CLOUDS

By Willma Willis Gore

When I was about ten years old, my maternal grandmother came for her regular two-month visit. I treasured my time with her. She always treated me as though I were capable of under-standing whatever she told me—even though I often did not comprehend the philosophical ideas she shared.

My most unforgettable exchange with her brought me a truth that has been an inspiration to me all of my life. We were sitting on the front porch watching the sun set over the mountains on the west side of the narrow valley where we lived. Clouds had gathered at the top of the opposite range—pink, lavender, and white. They changed shapes as we watched.

Grandmother gestured toward the clouds. "See how beautiful they are," she said.

"Yes, Grandma, they are beautiful. One looks like a pink zeppelin."

She turned to me and said in solemn tones, "Enjoy seeing them and treasure the sight, because no matter how many times you see beautiful clouds, you will never again in your lifetime see them in exactly the same shape and size and color as you see them now."

She took my hand in hers and looked deep into my eyes. "And you are like those clouds. You are the only person in the world exactly like you and the only one who will ever be exactly like you."

This was a profound thought to me then and remains so now. More than anything else in my childhood years, it inspired me to do the best I could with whatever gifts I have been given and to pick up the pieces and go on whenever I fell flat on my face—and I have fallen many times. I have always managed to get up from a fall remembering that I am the only one responsible for my life and the one responsible to make it the best I possibly can. Those few words from Grandmother have been my "life jacket" through years of stormy seas.

My last visit with her took place when I was an adult. She was in bed at the home of my aunt, an oxygen tank beside her. A thin tube brought the life support to her body. Her eyes sparkled and she held a book in her hand. She had always told me that life was a great adventure that did not end with death. The "passing of this body" just meant a transition to the next grand adventure. But when I went into the room, she greeted me cheerfully. "Willma," she said, "you must read this book. It has some wonderful ideas." She died three days later.

Needless to say, her attitude toward life and her encouragement of my dreams have remained a powerful influence to me, and now in my eighty-fourth year, I, too, look forward to the next grand adventure. I'm sure she will be there to "show me the ropes."[8]

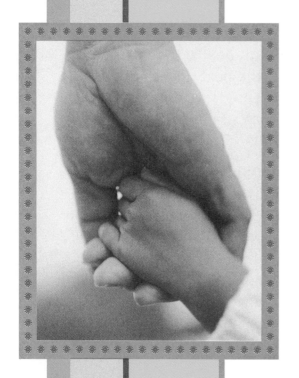

When God created Grandmas,

He mixed unconditional love

with unlimited patience,

unflappable faith with amazing

wisdom, and eternal hope

with undying commitment.

F. NEWTON

GRANDMAS ARE FOR HUGGING

Grandmas are for hugging
    When grandkids need a hug.
Grandmas are for baking
    With grandkids' apron tug.
Grandmas are for listening
    To all your secret dreams.
Grandmas are for praying
    When life is bad, it seems.

VICTORIA CRANK

*Your love has given me great
joy and encouragement.*

PHILEMON 1:7

✳ ✳ ✳ ✳ ✳

Heavenly Father,

I know You have a special plan in mind for each of my grand-children. Even now, You're uniquely suiting each of them with the talents, skills, and desires that will make it possible for them to excel and find joy in the tasks You're calling them to.

I pray that they would enjoy this time of learning new skills, developing their talents, and discovering Your purpose for their lives. As they grow older and face important decisions about the future, may they be motivated by a desire to find Your perfect plan for them rather than by the desires of others or a love of money.

As their grandma, give me wisdom to know how to help them along in this process. I want to encourage them to dream big and to trust You to take care of those areas in which they may not feel capable. Thank You for inspiring our hearts with great dreams and for making those dreams a reality.

Amen.

I THANK GOD for you, GRANDMA.

You always ENCOURAGE me to dream!

You're the

BEST

GRANDMA

in the World Because...

You Lovingly Share
Your Faith.

My grandmother's greatest gift

to me was her faith.

LACEE BROWN

✻ ✻ ✻ ✻ ✻ ✻ ✻ ✻ ✻ ✻ ✻ ✻ ✻ ✻ ✻ ✻ ✻ ✻ ✻ ✻

Praise be to the God and Father of our Lord Jesus Christ!
In his great mercy he has given us new birth into a living hope through
the resurrection of Jesus Christ from the dead, and into an inheritance
that can never perish, spoil or fade—kept in heaven for you.

1 PETER 1:3–4

Far greater than any material gift you could give to your grandchildren is your legacy of faith. If you aren't already doing it, take every opportunity you are given to share with them your relationship with God. When they visit, make sure prayer is a part of your daily routine. When you read to them, include some Bible stories appropriate for their ages. Talk openly about your faith around them, and listen for opportunities to help them learn about God through the questions they ask you.

They will grow out of the toys and clothes you give them, and any material inheritance you leave them will not last forever. But the message of God's love you share with them will stay with them throughout their lives on earth and will follow them on into eternity.

✻ ✻ ✻ ✻ ✻ ✻ ✻ ✻ ✻ ✻ ✻ ✻ ✻ ✻ ✻ ✻ ✻ ✻ ✻ ✻

A LETTER TO MY GRANDMA

Dear Grandma,

Your faith is such a part of who you are, I can't think about you without being reminded of your loving relationship with God. When you fix a meal for us, you always bless it with prayer. When you're working in your garden, you talk about the marvels of God's creation. All of our conversations, no matter how varied the topics, always come back to a scripture verse you've recently read or a thought about God's wonderful love for us.

Thank you, Grandma, for the many seeds of faith you've planted in my life. I want God to become as much a part of my life as He is of yours. I want my walk with Him to become as constant and natural as yours is. Thank you for the many ways you share your faith with others.

Love,

Your Grandchild

I want to love God

as much as my grandma

loves Him.

My Grandma is like one of God's angels.
She is always there to say, "Fear not."
She speaks God's Word often to my heart.

She is there to serve
With tenderhearted love,
And point to my heavenly Father above.

ELIZABETH CHARLETON

THE MOVIE TICKET

By Sally Clark

When I was a little girl, the biggest fear I had was that I was going to go to hell. I worried about it all the time. I thought about it when I was swinging high, my feet pushing into the clouds. I fretted about it when I sat in church, somber organ music filling my ears. And at night I lay awake, thinking about it while I stared out at a window full of stars, feeling very, very small.

One day I was looking through a family photo album with my grandmother. The people in the small black-and-white squares had died long before I was born.

Turning one of the pages, my grandma said, "Just think, Sally, someday you'll meet all of these people in heaven and get to know them."

That's when I got my courage up and asked, "Grandma, what if I go to hell instead of heaven when I die?"

Grandma stopped turning the pages and looked at me. "Do you believe that Jesus is your Savior, honey?" she asked.

"Of course I do, Gran," I answered, "but what if I go to hell anyway? What if I'm not good enough to go to heaven?"

My grandmother closed the album and pulled me onto her

lap. "Honey, do you remember last week when we went to the movies together?"

"Sure," I said. The week before, Gran had taken me to a movie that we both wanted to see. We had a great time there together. Grandma bought lemonade and popcorn for us to share. We laughed together at the funny parts and cried together when the movie was sad. When it was over, we walked out into the sunlight, blinking hard and holding hands.

"Do you know why you got to go to the movies, honey?" Gran asked.

"Because you took me," I answered.

"That's right," Gran said, hugging me tight. "You got to go to the movies because I took you there. I wanted you to go with me. I wanted us to be together because I love you." Gran kissed my cheek. "Do you remember who paid for the tickets?"

"You did, Gran. I don't have any money," I said, wiggling around to face her.

"That's right, honey," Gran said. "You got to go to the movies because I paid for your ticket. I love you, and I wanted us to be together. Now do you understand?"

"Understand what?"

"Understand why you're going to heaven instead of hell when you die," my grandmother explained. "You see, honey, the movie theater was like heaven to you. It was a place that you couldn't get into on your own, and I was like Jesus. I paid your way in when you couldn't, so that we could be together."

Feeling my grandmother's arms around me, I began to understand that I wasn't going to heaven because I was a good girl—I was going to go to heaven because Someone who loved me had bought my way there, just like my grandma had bought my ticket into the movie theater that day.

Now that I am grown, I understand so much more, but I still thank Jesus for buying my ticket and for giving me a grandma who could show me so clearly what He did for me.[9]

I will open my mouth
in parables,
I will utter hidden things,
things from of old—
what we have heard and known,
what our fathers have told us.
We will not hide them
from their children;
we will tell the next generation
the praiseworthy deeds
of the LORD,
his power, and the wonders
he has done.

PSALM 78:2–4

WHY I'M THANKFUL
YOU'RE MY GRANDMA . . .

. . . You showed me that God loves me—
even more than you do!

From everlasting to everlasting the
LORD's love is with those who fear him,
and his righteousness with their children's children.

PSALM 103:17

✳ ✳ ✳ ✳ ✳

Lord,

You know the desires of my heart, and You know that among the greatest of those desires is to be able to share eternity with my children and grandchildren in Your presence. I thank You for Your faithfulness in drawing my family to You and for those who have already placed their trust in You.

For those who have not yet made a decision to accept You as the Lord of their lives, I ask that You would continue to demonstrate Your unceasing love toward them. Place people in their lives who will point them toward a personal relationship with You.

Father, make me an instrument of Your love toward my family. Help me to seize every opportunity You place before me to share Your love and grace with my family. It's the most important thing I will do in this lifetime. Thank You for Your saving grace and Your unfailing love toward us.

Amen.

I THANK GOD for you, GRANDMA, for showing me GOD'S LOVE!

I LOVE VISITING
GRANDMA BECAUSE . . .

- She makes learning about God fun.

- She makes Mickey Mouse waffles from scratch, not the kind from the freezer.

- She plays games with me.

- She makes meat that's easy to chew.

- She listens to me read.

- She lets me drink soda pop.

- She lets me run in the house.

Ever since the day I was born,
you have nurtured me with love and kindness.
You have been someone I can believe in,
and someone I can depend upon
in this world I am just starting to understand,
and it's important to me that you know
how grateful I am
for all that you give to me,
for all that you teach me,
and for the strength I will always have,
because of you, Grandma.

Author Unknown

NOTES

[1] Sally Clark, Fredericksburg, Texas. Story used by permission of author.
[2] Robert Wall, Eau Claire, Wisconsin. Story used by permission of author.
[3] Jeremy Moore, Turnersville, New Jersey. Story used by permission of author.
[4] Alice Malloy, Long Island, New York. Story used by permission of author.
[5] Donna J. Shepherd, Middletown, Ohio. Story used by permission of author.
[6] Renie Burghardt, Doniphan, Missouri. Story used by permission of author.
[7] Carrie Younce, Escondido, California. Story used by permission of author.
[8] Willma Willis Gore, Sedona, Arizona. Story used by permission of author.
[9] Sally Clark, Fredericksburg, Texas. Story used by permission of author.

LOOK FOR THESE BOOKS:

THE BEST FRIEND
IN THE WORLD

THE BEST SISTER
IN THE WORLD

THE BEST TEACHER
IN THE WORLD

HOWARD BOOKS
A DIVISION OF SIMON & SCHUSTER
New York   London   Toronto   Sydney